I AM GRATEFUL

Always be grateful!

AUTHOR
CELIA KIBLER

ILLUSTRATOR
ROCIO MONROY

Published Proudly in the United States of America
Copyright ©Celia Kibler 2020
All rights reserved.

This book cannot be copied, resold or redistributed without prior consent of its author.

I AM GRATEFUL FOR TREES,
I HAVE A GREAT PLACE TO CLIMB

I AM GRATEFUL FOR CLOCKS,
TO TELL ME THE TIME.

I AM GRATEFUL
FOR DIRTY DISHES,
MEANS I HAVE FOOD TO EAT.

I AM GRATEFUL FOR SIDEWALKS, SO I DON'T WALK IN THE STREET.

I AM GRATEFUL FOR WINDOWS, BECAUSE I CAN LOOK OUT AND SEE.

I AM GRATEFUL FOR HONEY,
THAT COMES FROM A BEE.

I AM GRATEFUL FOR SCHOOL, SO I CAN LEARN SOMETHING NEW.

I AM GRATEFUL FOR TEETH,
BECAUSE THEY HELP ME CHEW.

I AM GRATEFUL FOR SIRENS, BECAUSE HELP IS ON THE WAY!

I AM GRATEFUL FOR SNOW,
SO I CAN RIDE ON MY SLEIGH.

I AM GRATEFUL FOR LAUNDRY, SHOWS I HAVE CLOTHES TO WEAR.

I AM GRATEFUL FOR FANS, BECAUSE THEY BLOW AROUND AIR.

I AM GRATEFUL FOR BOOKS,
FILLED WITH PLACES TO GO,

I AM GRATEFUL FOR BALLS, THEY'RE SO FUN TO THROW.

I AM GRATEFUL WHEN MOM,
SAYS TO STRAIGHTEN MY BED,
'CAUSE IT'S MY SPECIAL PLACE,
WHERE I LAY MY HEAD.

I AM GRATEFUL FOR MY MOUTH,
AND MY REALLY BIG SMILE,

I AM GRATEFUL FOR FRIENDS, WHEN THEY STAY FOR A WHILE.

I AM SO VERY GRATEFUL,
FOR MY FATHER AND MOTHER,

I AM GRATEFUL FOR MY FAMILY, 'CAUSE WE LOVE EACH OTHER.

WHAT ARE YOU GRATEFUL FOR?

_____

_____

_____

_____

_____

About the Author

Celia Kibler is the Author of RAISING HAPPY TODDLERS: How to Gain Great Parenting Skills and Stop Yelling at Your Kids. Her children's books include Being Different is Fun, All About Me and I Am Grateful. She is the Founder of Pumped Up Parenting (2016) and Funfit® Family Fitness (1987).

Celia is the Mom of 5 kids; 2 she gave birth to & 3 she gained from marriage; as well as a Grandma of 9. She has successfully parented a blended family for over 24 years.

As a Family Empowerment Coach, Celia is on a Mission to stop 1,000,000 parents from yelling at their kids and specializes in creating cooperative childhoods that everyone in the family can blossom from.

Celia has always believed that gratitude will change attitudes from entitled to appreciative. Being grateful through life will keep you understanding how fortunate you are in a world that focuses too much on getting more and more materialistic things.

Celia has always stood by her belief that the best things in life aren't things at all and writing this book gives her the opportunity to help children and parents to see the sparkle that exists in our everyday existence.

With over 40 years of coaching, teaching, counseling kids and their parents, including Special Needs populations, Celia's love for children is evident in every aspect of her life.

She truly loves to rhyme (to the point that it drives her own kids a little crazy), but this gift and her understanding of how children's minds work, has led her to write many children's books that are yet to come.

Connect with Celia on all Social Media outlets... YT, FB, IG, LI, Pinterest

celia@celiakibler.com
www.CeliaKibler.com
www.PumpedUpParenting.com
www.Funfit.com

More books by Celia Kibler
available on Amazon

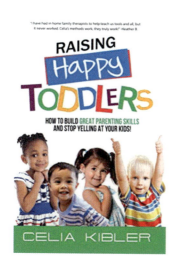

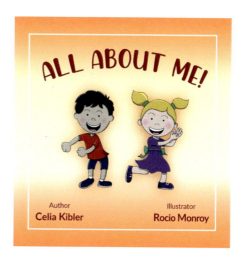

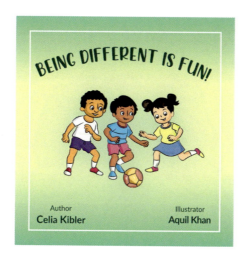

Made in the USA
Columbia, SC
14 February 2022